W. A. Mozart
Menuet, from String Quartet in D minor, K. 421

Of the twenty-three quartets which Mozart wrote in his short life, no. 15 in D minor was one of the six dedicated to Haydn and written with motivation from within rather than from a commission. These quartets (beginning with no. 14 in G major, K. 387) are important contributions to the development of chamber music. They mark Mozart's stylistic maturity, displaying thematic development and harmonic originality at new heights. Haydn's influence is evident, particularly from the standpoint of each voice sharing in the development of the musical ideas. The D minor quartet was finished just six months after the first, in June, of 1783, coinciding with the birth of Mozart's first child, and was published in 1785.

The third movement of the quartet (arranged here for woodwind quintet) is marked Allegretto and is in the typical Menuet-Trio-DaCapo form. The first section (Menuet) is in D minor in small ternary form while the Trio is in the parallel major, D, also a small ternary. The return of the Menuet (D.C.) is without repeats.

Josef Haydn
Introduction and Allegro

Haydn was already studying clavier and violin while a choirboy at St. Stephen's Cathedral in Vienna when he was only eight years old. All of his formal training came from the composer and voice teacher, Niccolo Porpora. In 1761, Haydn went into the employ of Prince Esterhazy as Kapellmeister. Performing themes of this position, he composed symphonies for the court orchestra and a great many chamber works, including string quartets and piano trios (piano, violin, and cello). One of these *Klaviertrio*, in C major, is arranged here for woodwind quintet. It begins with a four measure Introduction, marked Adagio, forte. The Allegro is the main body of the movement and is in sonata-allegro form. The first theme is in the tonic while a bridge leads to the second theme and codetta in the dominant. A tutti rest, a Haydn characteristic, immediately precedes the development section which begins with the flute and modulates through related keys until the dominant is reestablished. The recapitulation returns the themes somewhat modified and in C major. An extended coda serves as an additional development and brings the movement to a close on a fortissimo C major chord.

Adolphe Deslandres
Allegro, from Three Pieces for Quintette

An organist of some repute, Adolphe Edouard Marie Deslandres studied composition at the Paris Conservatoire under Leborne and Benoist. Several prizes were awarded his composition efforts, but none of his music has really survived the test of time. In 1862, he was appointed organist at Ste. Marie des Batignolles, a post he apparently held until the end of his musical career. He was diverse in his compositions which included three light operas: "Dimanche et Lundi" (1872), "Le Chevalier Bijou" (1875), and "Fridolin" (1876); patriotic dirges, masses, cantatas, sacred choruses; an oratorio, and many songs. His contribution to wind music is best exemplified by Trois Pieces en Quintette for woodwind quintet, dedicated to the Modern Society of Wind Instruments.

The Allegro is the finale of the three short movements. Basically in two parts of two sections each, it opens in E minor with a 16 bar introduction, interrupted by two fermati, and again introduces the second part. The main thematic idea of each section is a marchlike expansion of a simple tune. A contrasting, lyrical theme follows the first section and returns again in E major before the codetta and close, reminiscent of the introduction, in E minor.

Franz D
Windquintet in G mir

The orchestra at the Electoral Cou renowned all over Europe for its impressive abilities. Superbly trained by the composer Stamitz, the orchestra could produce a contrast of dynamics and nuances which had never been heard before. It was to this orchestra that the Italian cellist, Innocente Danzi, came in 1754 as first cellist and continued in this post until his death in 1783, when his son, Franz, succeeded him. A student of his father and of Vogler, Franz Danzi first became known as a composer *Singspiele* for the German national theater established in Mannheim. He became assistant-conductor after the Electorate had moved to Munich, but retired after the death of his wife, the famous opera singer Margarite Marchard, in 1800. However, in 1807 he took on the post of court conductor at Stuttgart, moving, in 1812, to a similar post at Carlsruhe where he remained until his death.

During his life time as a composer, he was principally known as an opera composer. As a teacher at Stuttgart, he had among his students, Carl Maria von Weber, the first German romanticist. In addition to his operas, Danzi wrote an oratorio and much music for the church. His experience at Mannheim (and later Munich) gave rise to an output of instrumental music including eight symphonies and 50 works for chamber ensembles. The Quintet for woodwinds, Op. 56, No. 2, was reprinted and is contained in Vol. XV, *D.T.B.*

In four movements, the G minor Quintet follows the typical instrumental forms of early classicism. The first movement, Allegretto, is a small sonata-allegro, the exposition in G minor and the recapitulation in G major. The Andante second movement, in 6-8 meter, is a ternary form in Eb major. The key of G minor returns in the third movement, Menuett and Trio, in a straight forward A-B-Da Capo with the Trio (B) in the parallel major. The Finale is marked Allegro, begins in G minor and ends in G major. The most virtuosic of the four movements, it is conceived as a modified ternary form.

Menuet, by C. M. Colomer

Except for the fact that he was Paris Conservatoire trained in the first quarter of this century, Colomer's lack of stature in the field of composition leaves no information on his life or contributions. His style of composition is in a very conservative 19th century manner, and this Menuet may be considered a good example of his tuneful but otherwise unimaginative and limited output.

The Menuet follows the more romantic technique of having a written rather than a Da Capo return of the opening themes. The A section is a small ternary in C major. The contrasting B (trio) section is in F major and is also a small ternary. The return is almost exactly the same as the opening section, also in C major and with the addition of a short, four measure codetta borrowed from the trio.

Notes by Hugo Magliocco

MMO CD 4603

Music Minus One

Bassoon Woodwind Music, Vol. 2

W.A. MOZART

MENUET
K. 421

Bassoon

5

JOSEPH HAYDN
Introduction & Allegro

MMO CD 4603

159

ADOLPHE DESLANDRES
Piece For Woodwind Quintet

MMO CD 4603

FRANZ DANZI

Woodwind Quintet in G minor
Opus 56, No. 2

COLOMER

MENUET

C.P.E. BACH
Andante
from Six Sonatas

3 taps (1 measure) precede music.

FRANZ JOSEPH HAYDN

Menuetto And Trio

from Octet

MMO CD 4603

PAUL KOEPKE

Rustic Holiday

4 taps (2 measures) precede music

CD 4603

W.A. MOZART
Andante and Country Dance
Divertimento No. 8, K.213

4 taps (2 measures) precede music

3 taps (1 1/2 measures) precede music

Country Dance E Rondeau

AUGUST KLUGHARDT

Andante Grazioso
from Quintet, Op.79

3 taps (1 measure) precede music

Andante grazioso

24

J.S. BACH

In Dulci Jobilo
from Das Orgelbüchlein

25

GUILLAUME BALAY

Petite Suite Miniature
No. 1 - Menuet

GUILLAUME BALAY
Edited by H. Voxman

3 taps (1 measure) precede music.

No. 2   Courte Gavotte

No. 3 - Sarabande

3 taps (1 measure) precede music.

* Observe fermata on D. C. only

No. 4 Petit Rondeau

W.A. MOZART
Allegro Molto
Divertimento No. 14, K.270

4 taps (1 measure) precede music.

Molto allegro

MMO CD 4603

MMO Compact Disc Catalog

BROADWAY

LES MISERABLES/PHANTOM OF THE OPERA	MMO CD 1016
HITS OF ANDREW LLOYD WEBBER	MMO CD 1054
GUYS AND DOLLS	MMO CD 1067
WEST SIDE STORY 2 CD Set	MMO CD 1100
CABARET 2 CD Set	MMO CD 1110
BROADWAY HEROES AND HEROINES	MMO CD 1121
CAMELOT	MMO CD 1173
BEST OF ANDREW LLOYD WEBBER	MMO CD 1130
THE SOUND OF BROADWAY	MMO CD 1133
BROADWAY MELODIES	MMO CD 1134
BARBRA'S BROADWAY	MMO CD 1144
JEKYLL & HYDE	MMO CD 1151
SHOWBOAT	MMO CD 1160
MY FAIR LADY 2 CD Set	MMO CD 1174
OKLAHOMA!	MMO CD 1175
THE SOUND OF MUSIC 2 CD Set	MMO CD 1176
SOUTH PACIFIC	MMO CD 1177
THE KING AND I	MMO CD 1178
FIDDLER ON THE ROOF 2 CD Set	MMO CD 1179
CAROUSEL	MMO CD 1180
PORGY AND BESS	MMO CD 1181
THE MUSIC MAN	MMO CD 1183
ANNIE GET YOUR GUN 2 CD Set	MMO CD 1186
HELLO DOLLY! 2 CD Set	MMO CD 1187
OLIVER 2 CD Set	MMO CD 1189
SUNSET BOULEVARD	MMO CD 1193
GREASE	MMO CD 1196
SMOKEY JOE'S CAFE	MMO CD 1197

CLARINET

MOZART CONCERTO, IN A	MMO CD 3201
WEBER CONCERTO NO. 1 IN FM. STAMITZ CON. NO. 3 IN BB	MMO CD 3202
SPOHR CONCERTO NO. 1 IN C MINOR OP. 26	MMO CD 3203
WEBER CONCERTO OP. 26, BEETHOVEN TRIO OP. 11	MMO CD 3204
FIRST CHAIR CLARINET SOLOS	MMO CD 3205
THE ART OF THE SOLO CLARINET:	MMO CD 3206
MOZART QUINTET IN A, K.581	MMO CD 3207
BRAHMS SONATAS OP. 120 NO. 1 & 2	MMO CD 3208
WEBER GRAND DUO CONCERTANT WAGNER ADAGIO	MMO CD 3209
SCHUMANN FANTASY OP. 73, 3 ROMANCES OP. 94	MMO CD 3210
EASY CLARINET SOLOS Volume 1 - STUDENT LEVEL	MMO CD 3211
EASY CLARINET SOLOS Volume 2 - STUDENT LEVEL	MMO CD 3212
EASY JAZZ DUETS - STUDENT LEVEL	MMO CD 3213
BEGINNING CONTEST SOLOS - Jerome Bunke, Clinician	MMO CD 3221
BEGINNING CONTEST SOLOS - Harold Wright	MMO CD 3222
INTERMEDIATE CONTEST SOLOS - Stanley Drucker	MMO CD 3223
INTERMEDIATE CONTEST SOLOS - Jerome Bunke, Clinician	MMO CD 3224
ADVANCED CONTEST SOLOS - Stanley Drucker	MMO CD 3225
ADVANCED CONTEST SOLOS - Harold Wright	MMO CD 3226
INTERMEDIATE CONTEST SOLOS - Stanley Drucker	MMO CD 3227
ADVANCED CONTEST SOLOS - Stanley Drucker	MMO CD 3228
ADVANCED CONTEST SOLOS - Harold Wright	MMO CD 3229

PIANO

BEETHOVEN CONCERTO NO 1 IN C	MMO CD 3001
BEETHOVEN CONCERTO NO. 2 IN Bb	MMO CD 3002
BEETHOVEN CONCERTO NO. 3 IN C MINOR	MMO CD 3003
BEETHOVEN CONCERTO NO. 4 IN G	MMO CD 3004
BEETHOVEN CONCERTO NO. 5 IN Eb (2 CD SET)	MMO CD 3005
GRIEG CONCERTO IN A MINOR OP.16	MMO CD 3006
RACHMANINOFF CONCERTO NO. 2 IN C MINOR	MMO CD 3007
SCHUMANN CONCERTO IN A MINOR	MMO CD 3008
BRAHMS CONCERTO NO. 1 IN D MINOR (2 CD SET)	MMO CD 3009
CHOPIN CONCERTO NO. 1 IN E MINOR OP. 11	MMO CD 3010
MENDELSSOHN CONCERTO NO. 1 IN G MINOR	MMO CD 3011
MOZART CONCERTO NO. 9 IN Eb K.271	MMO CD 3012
MOZART CONCERTO NO. 12 IN A K.414	MMO CD 3013
MOZART CONCERTO NO. 20 IN D MINOR K.466	MMO CD 3014
MOZART CONCERTO NO. 23 IN A K.488	MMO CD 3015
MOZART CONCERTO NO. 24 IN C MINOR K.491	MMO CD 3016
MOZART CONCERTO NO. 26 IN D K.537, CORONATION	MMO CD 3017
MOZART CONCERTO NO. 17 IN G K.453	MMO CD 3018
LISZT CONCERTO NO. 1 IN Eb, WEBER OP. 79	MMO CD 3019
LISZT CONCERTO NO. 2 IN A, HUNGARIAN FANTASIA	MMO CD 3020
J.S. BACH CONCERTO IN F MINOR, J.C. BACH CON. IN Eb	MMO CD 3021
J.S. BACH CONCERTO IN D MINOR	MMO CD 3022
HAYDN CONCERTO IN D	MMO CD 3023
HEART OF THE PIANO CONCERTO	MMO CD 3024
THEMES FROM GREAT PIANO CONCERTI	MMO CD 3025
TSCHAIKOVSKY CONCERTO NO. 1 IN Bb MINOR	MMO CD 3026
ART OF POPULAR PIANO PLAYING, Vol. 1 STUDENT LEVEL	MMO CD 3033
ART OF POPULAR PIANO PLAYING, Vol. 2 STUDENT LEVEL 2 CD Set	MMO CD 3034
'POP' PIANO FOR STARTERS STUDENT LEVEL	MMO CD 3035
MOZART COMPLETE MUSIC FOR PIANO FOUR HANDS 2 CD Set	MMO CD 3036

INSTRUCTIONAL METHODS

RUTGERS UNIVERSITY MUSIC DICTATION/EAR TRAINING COURSE (7 CD Set)	MMO CD 7001
EVOLUTION OF THE BLUES	MMO CD 7004
THE ART OF IMPROVISATION, VOL. 1	MMO CD 7005
THE ART OF IMPROVISATION, VOL. 2	MMO CD 7006
THE BLUES MINUS YOU Ed Xiques, Soloist	MMO CD 7007

VIOLIN

BRUCH CONCERTO NO. 1 IN G MINOR OP.26	MMO CD 3100
MENDELSSOHN CONCERTO IN E MINOR	MMO CD 3101
TSCHAIKOVSKY CONCERTO IN D OP. 35	MMO CD 3102
BACH DOUBLE CONCERTO IN D MINOR	MMO CD 3103
BACH CONCERTO IN A MINOR, CONCERTO IN E	MMO CD 3104
BACH BRANDENBURG CONCERTI NOS. 4 & 5	MMO CD 3105
BACH BRANDENBURG CONCERTO NO. 2, TRIPLE CONCERTO	MMO CD 3106
BACH CONCERTO IN DM, (FROM CONCERTO FOR HARPSICHORD)	MMO CD 3107
BRAHMS CONCERTO IN D OP. 77	MMO CD 3108
CHAUSSON POEME, SCHUBERT RONDO	MMO CD 3109
LALO SYMPHONIE ESPAGNOLE	MMO CD 3110
MOZART CONCERTO IN D K.218, VIVALDI CON. AM OP.3 NO.6	MMO CD 3111
MOZART CONCERTO IN A K.219	MMO CD 3112
WIENIAWSKI CON. IN D. SARASATE ZIGEUNERWEISEN	MMO CD 3113
VIOTTI CONCERTO NO.22	MMO CD 3114
BEETHOVEN 2 ROMANCES, SONATA NO. 5 IN F "SPRING SONATA"	MMO CD 3115
SAINT-SAENS INTRODUCTION & RONDO,	
MOZART SERENADE K. 204, ADAGIO K.261	MMO CD 3116
BEETHOVEN CONCERTO IN D OP. 61(2 CD SET)	MMO CD 3117
THE CONCERTMASTER	MMO CD 3118
AIR ON A G STRING Favorite Encores with Orchestra Easy Medium	MMO CD 3119
CONCERT PIECES FOR THE SERIOUS VIOLINIST Easy Medium	MMO CD 3120
18TH CENTURY VIOLIN PIECES	MMO CD 3121
ORCHESTRAL FAVORITES - Volume 1 - Easy Level	MMO CD 3122
ORCHESTRAL FAVORITES - Volume 2 - Medium Level	MMO CD 3123
ORCHESTRAL FAVORITES - Volume 3 - Med to Difficult Level	MMO CD 3124
THE THREE B'S BACH/BEETHOVEN/BRAHMS	MMO CD 3125
VIVALDI Concerto in A Minor Op. 3 No. 6. in D Op. 3 No. 9.	
Double Concerto Op. 3 No. 8	MMO CD 3126
VIVALDI-THE FOUR SEASONS (2 CD Set)	MMO CD 3127
VIVALDI Concerto in Eb, Op. 8, No. 5. ALBINONI Concerto in A	MMO CD 3128
VIVALDI Concerto in E, Op. 3, No. 12. Concerto in C Op. 8, No. 6 "Il Piacere"	MMO CD 3129
SCHUBERT Three Sonatinas	MMO CD 3130
HAYDN String Quartet Op. 76 No. 1	MMO CD 3131
HAYDN String Quartet Op. 76 No. 2	MMO CD 3132
HAYDN String Quartet Op. 76 No. 3 "Emperor"	MMO CD 3133
HAYDN String Quartet Op. 76 No. 4 "Sunrise"	MMO CD 3134
HAYDN String Quartet Op. 76 No. 5	MMO CD 3135
HAYDN String Quartet Op. 76 No. 6	MMO CD 3136
BEAUTIFUL MUSIC FOR TWO VIOLINS 1st position, vol. 1	MMO CD 3137
BEAUTIFUL MUSIC FOR TWO VIOLINS 2nd position, vol. 2	MMO CD 3138
BEAUTIFUL MUSIC FOR TWO VIOLINS 3rd position, vol. 3	MMO CD 3139
BEAUTIFUL MUSIC FOR TWO VIOLINS 1st, 2nd, 3rd position, vol. 4	MMO CD 3140
BARTOK: 44 DUETS	MMO CD 3141

Lovely folk tunes and selections from the classics, chosen for their melodic beauty and technical value.
They have been skillfully transcribed and edited by Samuel Applebaum, one of America's foremost teachers.

CELLO

DVORAK Concerto in B Minor Op. 104 (2 CD Set)	MMO CD 3701
C.P.E. BACH Concerto in A Minor	MMO CD 3702
BOCCHERINI Concerto in Bb, BRUCH Kol Nidrei	MMO CD 3703
TEN PIECES FOR CELLO	MMO CD 3704
SCHUMANN Concerto in Am & Other Selections	MMO CD 3705
CLAUDE BOLLING Suite For Cello & Jazz Piano Trio	MMO CD 3706

OBOE

ALBINONI Concerti in Bb, Op. 7 No. 3, No. 6, Dm Op. 9 No. 2.	MMO CD 3400
TELEMANN Conc. in Fm; HANDEL Conc. in Bb; VIVALDI Conc.in Dm	MMO CD 3401
MOZART Quartet in F K.370, STAMITZ Quartet in F Op. 8 No. 3	MMO CD 3402
BACH Brandenburg Concerto No. 2, Telemann Con. in Am	MMO CD 3403
CLASSIC SOLOS FOR OBOE Delia Montenegro, Soloist	MMO CD 3404

GUITAR

BOCCHERINI Quintet No. 4 in D "Fandango"	MMO CD 3601
GIULIANI Quintet in A Op. 65	MMO CD 3602
CLASSICAL GUITAR DUETS	MMO CD 3603
RENAISSANCE & BAROQUE GUITAR DUETS	MMO CD 3604
CLASSICAL & ROMANTIC GUITAR DUETS	MMO CD 3605
GUITAR AND FLUTE DUETS Volume 1	MMO CD 3606
GUITAR AND FLUTE DUETS Volume 2	MMO CD 3607
BLUEGRASS GUITAR CLASSIC PIECES minus you	MMO CD 3608
GEORGE BARNES GUITAR METHOD Lessons from a Master	MMO CD 3609
HOW TO PLAY FOLK GUITAR 2 CD Set	MMO CD 3610
FAVORITE FOLKS SONGS FOR GUITAR	MMO CD 3611
FOR GUITARS ONLY! Jimmy Raney Small Band Arrangements	MMO CD 3612
TEN DUETS FOR TWO GUITARS Geo. Barnes/Carl Kress	MMO CD 3613
PLAY THE BLUES GUITAR A Dick Weissman Method	MMO CD 3614
ORCHESTRAL GEMS FOR CLASSICAL GUITAR	MMO CD 3615

BANJO

BLUEGRASS BANJO Classic & Favorite Banjo Pieces	MMO CD 4401
PLAY THE FIVE STRING BANJO Vol. 1 Dick Weissman Method	MMO CD 4402
PLAY THE FIVE STRING BANJO Vol. 2 Dick Weissman Method	MMO CD 4403

FLUTE

MOZART Concerto No. 2 in D, QUANTZ Concerto in G	MMO CD 3300
MOZART Concerto in G K.313	MMO CD 3301
BACH Suite No. 2 in B Minor	MMO CD 3302

MMO Compact Disc Catalog

BOCCHERINI Concerto in D, VIVALDI Concerto in G Minor "La Notte",
MOZART Andante for Strings ....MMO CD 3303
HAYDN Divertimento, VIVALDI Concerto in D Op. 10 No. 3 "Bullfinch",
FREDERICK THE GREAT Concerto in C ....MMO CD 3304
VIVALDI Conc. in F; TELEMANN Conc. in D; LECLAIR Conc. in C ....MMO CD 3305
BACH Brandenburg No. 2 in F, HAYDN Concerto in D ....MMO CD 3306
BACH Triple Concerto, VIVALDI Concerto in D Minor ....MMO CD 3307
MOZART Quartet in F, STAMITZ Quartet in F ....MMO CD 3308
HAYDN 4 London Trios for 2 Flutes & Cello ....MMO CD 3309
BACH Brandenburg Concerti Nos. 4 & 5 ....MMO CD 3310
MOZART 3 Flute Quartets in D, A and C ....MMO CD 3311
TELEMANN Suite in A Minor, GLUCK Scene from 'Orpheus',
PERGOLESI Concerto in G   2 CD Set ....MMO CD 3312
FLUTE SONG: Easy Familiar Classics ....MMO CD 3313
VIVALDI Concerti In D, G, and F ....MMO CD 3314
VIVALDI Concerti in A Minor, G, and D ....MMO CD 3315
EASY FLUTE SOLOS Beginning Students   Volume 1 ....MMO CD 3316
EASY FLUTE SOLOS Beginning Students   Volume 2 ....MMO CD 3317
EASY JAZZ DUETS   Student Level ....MMO CD 3318
FLUTE & GUITAR DUETS   Volume 1 ....MMO CD 3319
FLUTE & GUITAR DUETS   Volume 2 ....MMO CD 3320
BEGINNING CONTEST SOLOS Murray Panitz ....MMO CD 3321
BEGINNING CONTEST SOLOS Donald Peck ....MMO CD 3322
INTERMEDIATE CONTEST SOLOS Julius Baker ....MMO CD 3323
INTERMEDIATE CONTEST SOLOS Donald Peck ....MMO CD 3324
ADVANCED CONTEST SOLOS Murray Panitz ....MMO CD 3325
ADVANCED CONTEST SOLOS Julius Baker ....MMO CD 3326
INTERMEDIATE CONTEST SOLOS Donald Peck ....MMO CD 3327
ADVANCED CONTEST SOLOS Murray Panitz ....MMO CD 3328
INTERMEDIATE CONTEST SOLOS Julius Baker ....MMO CD 3329
BEGINNING CONTEST SOLOS Doriot Anthony Dwyer ....MMO CD 3330
INTERMEDIATE CONTEST SOLOS Doriot Anthony Dwyer ....MMO CD 3331
ADVANCED CONTEST SOLOS Doriot Anthony Dwyer ....MMO CD 3332
FIRST CHAIR SOLOS with Orchestral Accompaniment ....MMO CD 3333

RECORDER

PLAYING THE RECORDER Folk Songs of Many Naitons ....MMO CD 3337
LET'S PLAY THE RECORDER Beginning Children's Method ....MMO CD 3338
YOU CAN PLAY THE RECORDER Beginning Adult Method ....MMO CD 3339

FRENCH HORN

MOZART Concerti No. 2 & No. 3 in Eb. K. 417 & 447 ....MMO CD 3501
BAROQUE BRASS AND BEYOND ....MMO CD 3502
MUSIC FOR BRASS ENSEMBLE ....MMO CD 3503
MOZART Sonatas for Two Horns ....MMO CD 3504
BEGINNING CONTEST SOLOS Mason Jones ....MMO CD 3511
BEGINNING CONTEST SOLOS Myron Bloom ....MMO CD 3512
INTERMEDIATE CONTEST SOLOS Dale Clevenger ....MMO CD 3513
INTERMEDIATE CONTEST SOLOS Mason Jones ....MMO CD 3514
ADVANCED CONTEST SOLOS Myron Bloom ....MMO CD 3515
ADVANCED CONTEST SOLOS Dale Clevenger ....MMO CD 3516
INTERMEDIATE CONTEST SOLOS Mason Jones ....MMO CD 3517
ADVANCED CONTEST SOLOS Myron Bloom ....MMO CD 3518
INTERMEDIATE CONTEST SOLOS Dale Clevenger ....MMO CD 3519

TRUMPET

THREE CONCERTI: HAYDN, TELEMANN, FASCH ....MMO CD 3801
TRUMPET SOLOS Student Level Volume 1 ....MMO CD 3802
TRUMPET SOLOS Student Level Volume 2 ....MMO CD 3803
EASY JAZZ DUETS Student Level ....MMO CD 3804
MUSIC FOR BRASS ENSEMBLE Brass Quintets ....MMO CD 3805
FIRST CHAIR TRUMPET SOLOS with Orchestral Accompaniment ....MMO CD 3806
THE ART OF THE SOLO TRUMPET with Orchestral Accompaniment ....MMO CD 3807
BAROQUE BRASS AND BEYOND Brass Quintets ....MMO CD 3808
THE COMPLETE ARBAN DUETS all of the classic studies ....MMO CD 3809
SOUSA MARCHES PLUS BEETHOVEN, BERLIOZ, STRAUSS ....MMO CD 3810
BEGINNING CONTEST SOLOS Gerard Schwarz ....MMO CD 3811
BEGINNING CONTEST SOLOS Armando Ghitalla ....MMO CD 3812
INTERMEDIATE CONTEST SOLOS Robert Nagel, Soloist ....MMO CD 3813
INTERMEDIATE CONTEST SOLOS Gerard Schwarz ....MMO CD 3814
ADVANCED CONTEST SOLOS Robert Nagel, Soloist ....MMO CD 3815
ADVANCED CONTEST SOLOS Armando Ghitalla ....MMO CD 3816
INTERMEDIATE CONTEST SOLOS Gerard Schwarz ....MMO CD 3817
ADVANCED CONTEST SOLOS Robert Nagel, Soloist ....MMO CD 3818
ADVANCED CONTEST SOLOS Armando Ghilalla ....MMO CD 3819
BEGINNING CONTEST SOLOS Raymond Crisara ....MMO CD 3820
BEGINNING CONTEST SOLOS Raymond Crisara ....MMO CD 3821
INTERMEDIATE CONTEST SOLOS Raymond Crisara ....MMO CD 3822

TROMBONE

TROMBONE SOLOS Student Level Volume 1 ....MMO CD 3901
TROMBONE SOLOS Student Level Volume 2 ....MMO CD 3902
EASY JAZZ DUETS Student Level ....MMO CD 3903
BAROQUE BRASS & BEYOND Brass Quintets ....MMO CD 3904
MUSIC FOR BRASS ENSEMBLE Brass Quintets ....MMO CD 3905
BEGINNING CONTEST SOLOS Per Brevig ....MMO CD 3911
BEGINNING CONTEST SOLOS Jay Friedman ....MMO CD 3912
INTERMEDIATE CONTEST SOLOS Keith Brown, Professor, Indiana University ....MMO CD 3913
INTERMEDIATE CONTEST SOLOS Jay Friedman ....MMO CD 3914
ADVANCED CONTEST SOLOS Keith Brown, Professor, Indiana University ....MMO CD 3915

ADVANCED CONTEST SOLOS Per Brevig ....MMO CD 3916
ADVANCED CONTEST SOLOS Keith Brown, Professor, Indiana University ....MMO CD 3917
ADVANCED CONTEST SOLOS Jay Friedman ....MMO CD 3918
ADVANCED CONTEST SOLOS Per Brevig ....MMO CD 3919

DOUBLE BASS

BEGINNING TO INTERMEDIATE CONTEST SOLOS David Walter ....MMO CD 4301
INTERMEDIATE TO ADVANCED CONTEST SOLOS David Walter ....MMO CD 4302
FOR BASSISTS ONLY Ken Smith, Soloist ....MMO CD 4303
THE BEAT GOES ON Jazz - Funk, Latin, Pop-Rock ....MMO CD 4304

TENOR SAX

TENOR SAXOPHONE SOLOS Student Edition Volume 1 ....MMO CD 4201
TENOR SAXOPHONE SOLOS Student Edition Volume 2 ....MMO CD 4202
EASY JAZZ DUETS FOR TENOR SAXOPHONE ....MMO CD 4203
FOR SAXES ONLY Arranged by Bob Wilber ....MMO CD 4204

ALTO SAXOPHONE

ALTO SAXOPHONE SOLOS Student Edition Volume 1 ....MMO CD 4101
ALTO SAXOPHONE SOLOS Student Edition Volume 2. ....MMO CD 4102
EASY JAZZ DUETS FOR ALTO SAXOPHONE ....MMO CD 4103
FOR SAXES ONLY Arranged Bob Wilber ....MMO CD 4104
BEGINNING CONTEST SOLOS Paul Brodie, Canadian Soloist ....MMO CD 4111
BEGINNING CONTEST SOLOS Vincent Abato ....MMO CD 4112
INTERMEDIATE CONTEST SOLOS Paul Brodie, Canadian Soloist ....MMO CD 4113
INTERMEDIATE CONTEST SOLOS Vincent Abato ....MMO CD 4114
ADVANCED CONTEST SOLOS Paul Brodie. Canadian Soloist ....MMO CD 4115
ADVANCED CONTEST SOLOS Vincent Abato ....MMO CD 4116
ADVANCED CONTEST SOLOS Paul Brodie, Canadian Soloist ....MMO CD 4117
ADVANCED CONTEST SOLOS Vincent Abato ....MMO CD 4118

DRUMS

MODERN JAZZ DRUMMING 2 CD Set ....MMO CD 5001
FOR DRUMMERS ONLY ....MMO CD 5002
WIPE OUT ....MMO CD 5003
SIT-IN WITH JIM CHAPIN ....MMO CD 5004
DRUM STAR Trios/Quartets/Quintets Minus You ....MMO CD 5005
DRUMPADSTICKSKIN Jazz play-alongs with small groups ....MMO CD 5006
CLASSICAL PERCUSSION 2 CD Set ....MMO CD 5009
EIGHT MEN IN SEARCH OF A DRUMMER ....MMO CD 5010

VOCAL

SCHUBERT GERMAN LIEDER - High Voice, Volume 1 ....MMO CD 4001
SCHUBERT GERMAN LIEDER - Low Voice, Volume 1 ....MMO CD 4002
SCHUBERT GERMAN LIEDER - High Voice, Volume 2 ....MMO CD 4003
SCHUBERT GERMAN LIEDER - Low Voice, Volume 2 ....MMO CD 4004
BRAHMS GERMAN LIEDER - High Voice ....MMO CD 4005
BRAHMS GERMAN LIEDER - Low Voice ....MMO CD 4006
EVERYBODY'S FAVORITE SONGS - High Voice, Volume 1 ....MMO CD 4007
EVERYBODY'S FAVORITE SONGS - Low Voice, Volume 1 ....MMO CD 4008
EVERYBODY'S FAVORITE SONGS - High Voice, Volume 2 ....MMO CD 4009
EVERYBODY'S FAVORITE SONGS - Low Voice, Volume 2 ....MMO CD 4010
17th/18th CENT. ITALIAN SONGS - High Voice, Volume 1 ....MMO CD 4011
17th/18th CENT. ITALIAN SONGS - Low Voice, Volume 1 ....MMO CD 4012
17th/18th CENT. ITALIAN SONGS - High Voice, Volume 2 ....MMO CD 4013
17th/18th CENT. ITALIAN SONGS - Low Voice, Volume 2 ....MMO CD 4014
FAMOUS SOPRANO ARIAS ....MMO CD 4015
FAMOUS MEZZO-SOPRANO ARIAS ....MMO CD 4016
FAMOUS TENOR ARIAS ....MMO CD 4017
FAMOUS BARITONE ARIAS ....MMO CD 4018
FAMOUS BASS ARIAS ....MMO CD 4019
WOLF GERMAN LIEDER FOR HIGH VOICE ....MMO CD 4020
WOLF GERMAN LIEDER FOR LOW VOICE ....MMO CD 4021
STRAUSS GERMAN LIEDER FOR HIGH VOICE ....MMO CD 4022
STRAUSS GERMAN LIEDER FOR LOW VOICE ....MMO CD 4023
SCHUMANN GERMAN LIEDER FOR HIGH VOICE ....MMO CD 4024
SCHUMANN GERMAN LIEDER FOR LOW VOICE ....MMO CD 4025
MOZART ARIAS FOR SOPRANO ....MMO CD 4026
VERDI ARIAS FOR SOPRANO ....MMO CD 4027
ITALIAN ARIAS FOR SOPRANO ....MMO CD 4028
FRENCH ARIAS FOR SOPRANO ....MMO CD 4029
ORATORIO ARIAS FOR SOPRANO ....MMO CD 4030
ORATORIO ARIAS FOR ALTO ....MMO CD 4031
ORATORIO ARIAS FOR TENOR ....MMO CD 4032
ORATORIO ARIAS FOR BASS ....MMO CD 4033
BEGINNING SOPRANO SOLOS Kate Hurney ....MMO CD 4041
INTERMEDIATE SOPRANO SOLOS Kate Hurney ....MMO CD 4042
BEGINNING MEZZO SOPRANO SOLOS Fay Kittelson ....MMO CD 4043
INTERMEDIATE MEZZO SOPRANO SOLOS Fay Kittelson ....MMO CD 4044
ADVANCED MEZZO SOPRANO SOLOS Fay Kittelson ....MMO CD 4045
BEGINNING CONTRALTO SOLOS Carline Ray ....MMO CD 4046
BEGINNING TENOR SOLOS George Shirley ....MMO CD 4047
INTERMEDIATE TENOR SOLOS George Shirley ....MMO CD 4048
ADVANCED TENOR SOLOS George Shirley ....MMO CD 4049

BASSOON

SOLOS FOR THE BASSOON Janet Grice, Soloist ....MMO CD 4601